Greek Passages

Also by Peter Riley:

Poetry
Love-Strife Machine
The Canterbury Experimental Weekend
The Linear Journal
The Musicians, The Instruments
Preparations
Lines on the Liver
Tracks and Mineshafts
Ospita
Noon Province
Sea Watches
Reader
Lecture
Sea Watch Elegies
Royal Signals
Distant Points
Alstonefield
Between Harbours
Noon Province et autres poèmes
Snow has settled . . . bury me here
Author
Passing Measures: A Collection of Poems
The Sea's Continual Code
Aria with Small Lights
Alstonefield (extended edition)
Excavations
A Map of Faring
The Llŷn Writings
The Day's Final Balance: Uncollected Writings 1965–2006

Prose
Two Essays
Company Week
The Dance at Mociu

Peter Riley

Greek Passages
2002–2005

Shearsman Books
Exeter

Published in the United Kingdom in 2009 by
Shearsman Books Ltd
58 Velwell Road
Exeter EX4 4LD

www.shearsman.com

ISBN 978-1-84861-051-4

Copyright © Peter Riley, 2009.

The right of Peter Riley to be identified as the author of this work
has been asserted by him in accordance with the
Copyrights, Designs and Patents Act of 1988. All rights reserved.

Cover image copyright © Peter Riley.

Acknowledgements

Extracts from *Greek Passages* have appeared in *The Chicago Review, Fulcrum*, and the website magazines *Ahadada, Dusie, PoetryEtc* and *Masthead*.

The whole work in a slightly different version, can be heard read by the author, slowly and with interjections, on the website *Archive of the Now*.

Contents

ExoMáni 2002 (10 Preludes)   7

Argolid 2003
    I   20
    II   33
    III   47

Argolid 2004
    I   64
    II   77
    III   88

ExoMáni 2005 (10 Postludes)   103

Notes   118
Bibliography   120

there must have been children sleeping
in sweet abandonment
as the unknown sailed into the harbour
and the world stopped

Kelvin Corcoran

10 PRELUDES
EXOMÁNI 2002

There was no journey. The moment we opened our eyes we were there: / the colours across the bay / the red on the blue / Trinakrian Sea, its / turning islands, and all thought of betterment in the world / Bringing trouble. That lives here like a stone. / Bringing upright posture, anxiety, and longed-for repose. That live here like the flowers of the mountain.

•

At dawn, a white light on the top of a mountain / things start to move / an old woman side-flank on a donkey, at dawn / wobbling up the mountain, picking over the stones / a Mercedes glides past, the light there / in her eye ever shining // Slowness of the dawn beetle / western promise / worth goat-dung.

•

And at evening the sky falcon stands over the bay / sun sinking into meaning. The lights go on in the houses / A man gets out of a boat onto the stones of the shore, walks over to the bar / and is recognised / A jovial shout goes up / embracing everyone, our welcome / A treaty is caught in the moment, and brought on into the dance / Slim as pencils, the leaves / throw themselves at the music.

•

Thinking simple thoughts, like a dawn bird in my niche I / set forth, stepping lightly / walking the shoreline, testing the stability / of simple things, words, stones, against each other, the light radiating between sea and mountainside the air hot as blood / the very living blood that bears our histories.

•

Who was it, sailed from this harbour, who, / sailed out / together / Kelvin tell me / from this small harbour that time / deep in the power / We threw all our money into the sea // And what became of that / thing they call love / what powers massed what quiet graves / carried that emblem to the sides of the earth // Sea surface tensed out, ultra- / marine against the white walls, the wind ready, the boat edging out at the gap / everything we ever owned / flung at eternity.

•

The sea noise ringing in our ears / the return a cadence of the departure or the song thus broken. Always at that opening to the whitechapelled sea the spirit enters its turbulence, and / little owls on the electricity wires.

•

Something almost forgotten, making possible a dazzling sanity / A buzzard swoops over an abandoned monastery garden in the hills, like a jet passing. 'Whoosh!' / Keeping an eye on the fig tree // Gods came this way and scored the earth / with our amalgamated desires / each for all / and the stars, struggling all day to get out of the sea.

•

Caves in the coastal cliffs, pirate storage or homes of acolytes, now bricked up / Tortoises plodding around in the undergrowth below // The geology down the coast echoing / the treatises of light, waves of soft rock halting against the void // Swallow at the door, sun's red eye in the bay, compass leaves descending.

•

And such light I've never seen such light, all round us land and sea negotiating / over our blood, casting translucent banners across hard earth / Thin grey leaves fluttering, thunder in the hills, a new / wind across the harbour, the small boat setting out // The old women knitting in the alcove, keeping an eye on the mating rituals, threading the world into their harmony / The world watches, the small boat moving out across the wind / prow set for the world's end / for a year and a day. / Small chirruping cries, echoed along the coastal cliffs.

•

Sweetly then / the whole thing / complete and / sailing away, singing: *Noë noë noë* . . . // Sings shouting: new, new born. // Welcome home, little turnip, welcome to the old song.

Argolid 2003

I

Pulling the net onto the shore / the goods to market, and market fears, swallow so high / and market loves, the goods brought home / across the bottomless Lake of Lerna, great/ void in sense where monsters thrive, the Hydra on the skyline shaking her heads / now drained and producing purple aubergines.

•

Our sustenance dragged across our fear / purposeless gloom in half light / long fields of grey stalks pulled by the wind, our profit / hauled onto the land / up the long valley and into the hills // Turn and look back, strong hot wind in the face with some water in it, the olive trees thrashing / Our wealth, weighing, working, wearing us / on / to the empty monastery.

•

Elleniko, the watch tower, keeping an eye on the sea / A fleet of wooden ships approaches up the bay on the wind, bringing trouble / Fifty maidens breathing abhorrence, hotly pursued by fifty princes breathing possession / An enormous administrative problem. // Floating towns / as tall as the lower mountains, anchored against St Mark's and dwarfing it / A privileged position, and where to go next // Monetarist evangelism, dialectical negativism, scientific fundamentalism, consumes its own path where are the / binoculars there was a silent bird.

•

Silent that looks at us sideways and shifts / away behind the leaves / No reason to be scared, little / beauty, ringdove, deeper into the leaves, another / wave hits the stones, grey pitching into rose // O don't you see yon lonesome dove / sittin on yon ivy tree / he's mourning for his true love, and so shall we.

•

Advancing towards us / up the bay, Phoenician traders / The king's daughters walk down to the shore, to see the foreign goods. Trouble: / suicide, putrefaction, bulldozers / war, waving her heads over the wildered plain // *Trouble so long, been troubled so long trouble don't worry my mind* // Dark milky clouds settle on the bay / night comes from behind the mountains / we rest in perilous ease, at blood temperature / Revenge, my sweet poison.

•

Wind, waves, trade, our money / sits staring at us. / White concrete villas along the shore, with big open verandas trailing vine leaves, fish for sale at the boats / Again the white threshold, the old fears echoing in the distance / trouble hovering, and sheep bells in the hills. / / The light of our souls downcast / onto the stones of the shore / *Money, what have you done?*

•

Sheep bells in the hills, tuned to the shepherd's flute (they were 'very particular' about this) / I am ill, I lie on the bed, bad news comes in: / another Palestinian wedding party shelled, another / history denied / / Take up / that harmony, between particulars, to remember the slowness / of the light rising / in memory.

•

In memory of justice, the length of the night. An animal / runs past the window, probably a marten / earlier there was gunfire – / a wedding, as in Palestine, they fire guns in the air. Here it frightens the wildlife / / Death / pacing up the stone steps / the dark boat on the pale shore / the creak on the office carpet.

•

They died, as we all do, it / came up the bay at them / like a new song / /

·

Wake into fallen dark / the labyrinth cut into the open / White egrets, and the great white heron, on the dark shore / where they dump hard-core for the new discos. Palaces, megastores, always more than we need attack / the earth and the shy bird / takes wing // Wake into the question: what if nothing results? Would our biology keep us going? No, the mind / seeking itself strikes the shore / a stone turns / a tone returns.

•

A tone saying / Never mind, death had to come sooner or later. / Larkspur, wild gladiolus, and the orchid Ophrys bearing / signs of lamentation, the dark letter on the gay petal. And the squad at the watch tower signal another arrival, some new monstrosity / drifting up the bay / I have a bad cold, it was sent / as an aid to thought and observation. // Cyclamen, bright flags nodding among the dry stones. Seeking foreign partner.

•

The good ship sail on the alley-alley-o and a gradual understanding comes upon us / of transmission broken at fear, across the globe / Lady of the Lake, her / terrible heads / her fishy tail / calling back the dead in the new darkness // Flee this axis / go as far as you can before turning / three times round went she.

•

But you will turn, in the end / and look back across the silence waters, the / roaring gap // deep and wide, perfect justice / on the other side. Listen. Small bells.

II

Dear, we are in this small white house on the stony hillside / millipedes curled up on the walls like question marks / the great bay below and somebody calls / in the night / language seeming to grow out of the rock / like autumn cyclamen / 'A power, a concentration, a figure, a voice.'

•

A sound in the night, the dark uninhabited space of song / a Cycladic figure, on its back, suddenly has eyes, and opens them // Tell me what you see / The ceiling of the museum, why am I lying here in the night, so far from home / outside the world / there is no comfort.

•

Helen of the war, dig the grave here / *in far countree* // The church clock of Elleniko chimes on the half hour all day and all night. After midnight the next three chimes are identical, single stroke. // Helen this world lay before you, was it worth / a single thought? Her eyes thought so.

•

A great wave comes up the bay in the night carrying / sharpened coins / it breaks and dissolves against a stone chapel in the hills / wooden iconostasis / tuned to Radio Tarifa. // 'You can't love what you don't know', tracing the map of / England, in small love, her eyes / fought so.

•

Dear, I am so far, I am nobody, out in nowhere / millipedes curled up on the white walls like coiled springs / mulberry tree at the front door / A ringing in the night, what is that / / Phases of delight and alarm / coil round my heart when I / catch that music, / tuned to the distant hurt, the small voice.

•

Vulgar men our / impoverished vocabulary / our power handed to nobodies, pretences of men, unknowables / / The lights of Nafplio across the bay / from the shithouse window / divine interpreter / of my song.

•

O me it's / O my, what gone become of me, I used to fly high like a turtle dove, now all down town just hangin aroun . . . Uncle's song, dead relatives gathering round the house in the night. // *Last time I saw my maw and paw* they were in my dream and I was shouting at them You got no right, to come back / from what became of you.

•

Old dance-songs that sweep up their words from the floor / The old style of Cretan lyra with sympathetic strings running under the board, and pellet bells attached to the bow / The coin- and bell-hung dresses in the folk museum at Nafplio / Every move you make / is a guidance, and a pulsion / of the exchange // The extraordinary silence in the Dhofrion Gorge, from Élonas / above the vegetable fields of Leonídhi / A great fall of space / down past the trees in clefts of rock / a single thought / falls into the earth. Truth / rises into meaning / a nun trots past holding a basin of hot water.

•

The white rock eyrie, and all that space off the end of the line / shouting itself to nothing, in time to the sea. Echoing the plea. Take its hand, Susie Lee.

•

A quiet Sunday with slight rain, the old man plays his flute in his abandoned house down the fields / Can you hear me, advanced people? I know I am / very far away beyond the clouds / I'm telling you about Mr Vanghélis down the fields, the stone wall builder, the man with the sharpened senses, whose every action is a completed action, rounded, fulfilling its arc // I'm not asking anything for this. The winged archer / perches on my brow.

•

A mobile phone rings in the middle of the night /
Sudden bursts of wind like little tornadoes passing /
I don't make a narrative, I / await an arrival, a song.
// I'm getting to know this place: three steps down
turning half right / into the kitchen / in the night,
every window / showing coastal lights / Hello, yes,
what? / 'Christ is risen'. . . ?

•

The narrow shore behind Lerna, barely room to walk between the sea and the tall fences of the orange groves / Cloudy day on the stones / and suffering shall cease, and we all return to a pre-Aurignacian repletion / end all this / advance, torment. // There is no path, it ends / squeezed between land and sea / A dark town across the bay / Clumps of giant fennel, used in ancient times for carrying fire, the pith inflammable and long burning, we trust it and it / ends and we turn back, one by one it ends. // Roy Fisher hears me, up in the northern hills / and turns to pat / the dog that died.

•

Old steam locomotives rusting in the sidings at Mili / among eucalyptus trees, close to the sea / their couplings fall off, their doors are open / A small village with three bars, where youth pauses / An overwhelming / frustration and anger / a world emotion / lives in the cracks in the floor, making it difficult to dance.

•

There we wept / by the rivers / by the new software / exactly where / youth seeks change / by the electric fence, by the spring flowing into the sea, by the open arm / there.

III

We eat outside, under the lamp as it gets dark, in the company of moths. The lights of the bay gather at this end, as if pointing the way / towards Mycenae. // Lay down there, and rest, / exhausted by profit taking, close your eye.

•

All the big lies assembled at Mycenae. All the rights to live at the expense of others. // They took the old man's samovar, his one pleasure, in lieu of taxes, since he had nothing. For we hate the poor, and think they should pay for our dinners / Our credit with razor lips sings this song / *Lay you down and die.* // And the big stories came to Mycenae and wiped themselves against the stone walls.

•

Tales of snake spirits, that are repeated out of each other and don't know / which they are. They sit in the glass cases of the museum like Cumberland sausages waiting / for the millennium, for a narrative. // But four thousand years is nothing / common people commit such murders every day, the / nuthatch on the stone wall / lost in a wine of, a possible fullness. Streaked across the eye, secure for the day.

•

Kefalari. The water bursts out at the foot of the hill / which shall wash away these stories / Churches, and a lollipop kiosk, claim the place. Coachloads arrive wanting to buy something / something redemptive, though it might not last. // Up in the windy hills the rain / marginalises us, serving / every cell of the landscape.

•

The King of Asine has gone / Seferis too has gone. / The citadel, a boss of rock above the sea, the caravan park, and the massed hotels along the coast. / King, poet, a vertical thrust through all that horizontal continuity and steady cash. A clearing, a void, a cry across commerce, remembering honour, a citadel / with about enough grass among its stones to graze a donkey for a week as the sea diamonds shoot overhead // Come, little donkey, I'll hire you, for a year and a day / and you shall bear patiently a collection of CDs of rembetiko, demotika and Byzantine chant / in two wooden boxes along the coast road and across the vegetable fields 15km / to a semi-ruined stone house in from Iría which when we get there proves to have no electricity / But we know the tunes by heart, and sit in former time like little waves against cyclopean walls. Ten thousand years, drinking of the wine / Old poets, remembering the oceanic tones of a just peace.

•

Justice that survives in the tales while the actuality lies ten feet down a shaft grave. There was no justice. Tyrins, a fortress of privilege guarding the end of the bay and every advantage structure to be had. / Again the split brain advances, at someone's cost / The King so frightened he leapt into a large storage jar // Excavations under the summit palace, left partly open, reveal a Bronze Age circular structure divided into segments, the guide / was maybe drunk, didn't have much English and kept saying, "It is the marigold, you know, that little flower, it is the marigold."

·

We have our guides. Poetry guides, culture guides, war guides. They clear the path and take the fee. They expel the reactions and determine the causes. They know what is important. Greece, they tell us, was where farming entered Europe / Western men, they explain, want to rape eastern girls / A bit of resistance, they claim, is good for you. The keys of the piano are actually so stiff they can hardy be depressed at all and Greece entered Europe in 1923 singing *Yiá sou Lámbrou with your kanoún / O play that thing I've got / heartache and pain and I'm going to die / och, amán amán.*

•

Asia arrives constantly, by one way or another and all the mindless killers we send out / can't stop this flow, of desire / I lay my head / on the salt sea bed, and wake into / white sheets on my nostrils, the edge of light. / O take breath, open your eyes, they are all busy out there in the fields, Count Tolstoy in his smock.

•

The mind is a cold and lonely place, its doors locked. Outside in the moving air is where things happen. / The vast stone mountains of Greece, with fertile coastal strips and some high plateaux insufficient to support more than a few citadels run by killing machines, heroes of expansion and development. // The orange butterflies speckled black or brown, that vanished with the first rain.

•

We are out of favour, we are not in the know. We read books with titles like 'What, Then, Must We Do?' and 'Who is to Blame?' / We kick stones in the road / the dirt road that winds up into the hills, to the empty villages, the houses locked / or decayed / an erasure / across the forehead / the movement of clouds in the distance // The great redeemer, floating in the mind sad and cold saying, / 'A monumental trust lives in the heart.' / But there is an immediacy, a smoking chimney, somebody looks up from the news. The singing is unstoppable. A gecko runs across the wall-o.

•

I lie in bed dreaming the street plan / corners of dark northern towns, complex of small back streets I can't quite remember / My mother held my hand at the street edge / long ago, and we had our thin riches / there too, the future sailed up the bay as the potential, it seemed, of the entire land / held in the local hand // I dream this. Sound outside, swishing / of trees in gusts of wind / the red earth under the sky's black cloak / That I should come so far from such streets / rejoicing in the same fear.

•

It was Troy's turn / the surplus needed it. / We destroyed your house, helped ourselves to all the goods, cattle, women / though we got very little of it home. And what did arrive / at Mykines / sang of total loss so / full and sharply, we / stood confounded / while our governors / hanged themselves in pantie-hose shouting *Freedom and Democracy!*

•

Old socialists, I think we were trying to arrange for a bit of space around humanity, to breathe / in, to venture some trust, multiplying our senses of what we are . . . / / We are forgotten shoes in a shed / creaking irritating questions, about living off the labour of others / which everybody thinks is just great / We are reduced to a single moment, a shout of denial, a syllable in the night. Then we are finished.

•

Though my story is hardly begun / the white flower falls to the ground / the jay screeches across the fields, now freshly green in November / for this is Asia, and always has been. Here we live what we are / as a delicate garden, small blooms at the edge of the desert / invaded by ultramarine and the rosy pink cloud unfolding at the gates of dawn.

•

A reason for coming here. And dreaming in the night, of a steadfast resistance, and the joy and fear of belonging // The shout outside, its moment, as it encompasses us / taking us up into the entire landscape / of mutuality, shouted out onto the mountainside. Thus the double wings of the small brown moth on my arm, fluttering open in the breeze.

•

The Argive Heraion, the first place last. Vast arena of hills all round in low sunlight and the wind threshing the olive trees / A German tourist in shorts who walked from Mykines, the patient guardian in his hut watching television, everything / shaved down to a film on the earth / Power's monumental lock on sense / a smear of stone on a rise of ground. // Immense possibilities of breath. And, secured by distance from market serving, passionately affirmative.

ARGOLID **2004**

I

Again this house on a Greek hillside / Autumn. It is passion, not madness, the voices speaking through us / isn't it, Kelvin? The madness, you remember, Barry, / the revenge / tried to swallow the world and shattered all hope. / I think I know this place I / put out my hand in the dark for the door frame / I cut out my heart in the paper it might be serious. / I welcome myself back. I step out of the back door at night in my pyjamas, looking out over 20km of sea and mountain marked by small lights or none. Some kind of insane moth / flutters at my right ear / Learning the language.

•

Great curve of bay / great curve of disco bars, depot yards further back, heaps of old tourism clutter, separated by a perimeter fence and a bunch of reeds from the remains of the Lake of Lerna / Still water, choked, smoke rising beyond the westward horizon, and a bell ringing // An ancestral immunity to malaria (many-headed beast) among fishers and tenders of small water-mills, not shared with passing geographers and exiled dramatists . . . // Last juice of Mycenae trickling down from the hills, oil snake on the water what / form of world leads us out of this / what demography carries the soul westward / 'But if the entire Manifest of the world is absorbed / into gold, the world will be destroyed.' The disco bars are magnificent architectural fantasies in honour of the young heart bags of cash and great balls of fire.

•

Over the vegetable fields behind Iréa and up into the hills. Rise a few hundred feet and everything changes: dark conifers against white rock / To the 'Egg' Monastery at the end of a dirt track hanging over a small valley. No one at home. / *The knowledge that knows nothing, the empty room where brightness is born* / creeping through the narrow white corridors and cells, thick with grey dust, fallen plaster, at the centre a dark casket, a muscle that reflects the small lights, grips the world's fear and keeps silence / Lunch by the harbour at Vivari, watching kingfishers.

•

Pelei. Low white houses scattered on humps of bare earth, some of them closed up, some of them falling down. Among them a new tank, a bright white cube with a blue pipe attached. White hopes, some of them fallen. // 1913, rows of faces at a colonial boys' school in South Africa. A few of them can speak Xhona but they don't let it be known. / Buried hopes germinate. / To know the language, to learn the sayings: *Everything is for those who have none of it.*

•

Coming down that little road / to the sea near Mili that / calm, level, vast pool of light before us / horizonless, merged into the sky / Coming down that little road / & later walking the dark shore near the abandoned factory / A few waders in the shallows, perhaps a spoonbill. // How the money came and slopped around shouting 'New!' and was gone. Where did it go? / Debris scattered on the shore, and the bright white new apartment blocks, standing in the waste land like refrigerators, like sealed money-boxes. / Truth gathers together / the lines of the land the / forms of, tales of, melodies, of // That little, final, road. A heron standing knee-deep in the light, carefully studying it.

•

(Midea) Hilltop citadels, defended positions for the exploitation of areas of production on lower ground. Foreign stations, exacting 'tribute' on pain of punishment or erasure. And accumulating a surplus, of cash, of days, becoming 'civilised', exercising 'culture'. Expert horsemanship, expert cruelty, expert appetite. Art, another new block // and never gaining anything, living a frustrated anger that burns along the coast / and guides kings to their wreck.

•

Charming small Roman portrait busts in the museum at Astros. Wisps of hair behind the ears. A large tortoise crossing the main road near Xiropigádo, objects to being helped, hisses. / Points of confluence at which doors open, points tying memory to the route. Wisps of hair in marble like sea fossils. Small furrows in white glaze. / It is not nature / that needs guarding / it is us.

•

The rock thrush calling from the cliff. Lines of water curl round arms and shoulders. // The great hulk came floating up the bay, proclaiming itself in wild lights and amplified machine sounds, hotly pursued by 200 managers. 'We bring freedom and democracy.' We fled to the hills where the quotas are thin, and found employment, poor but direct, to return when trade had again become possible. They never knew that it was they who were going to be developed, to have their images straightened out, right here // Señor, ya estamas solos mi corazón y el mar Alone, my heart and the sea. Plural of 'alone'.

•

Gulf of Korinth

(1) Perachóra, the double sanctuary, the small ancient harbour emerging from scrub land, pink stone foundations in a nook of the coastline, hermit crabs under the pier, remains of a curved stoa overlooking the sea / To sit and talk in the cool of morning and evening: philosophers, those who discuss, and surmise, and let it pass / Ever open door, a place where people can take refuge, knowing that the sea traffic on the horizon will pass by. Here Medea killed her children. // What there might be clinging to the edges of the route, the great plain around Thebes now cotton fields, fluff in the margins of the road like snow, Asian stories ringing across the day. What might start up from the darkness. // Dhístomo and a hilltop mausoleum. June 10th 1944: 232 males aged 2 to 90. Classed as rural-asiatic disposables. A wall of glass-fronted wooden boxes. Baby skull like a hatched egg. // As the light dims, a bleak cross-roads among hill slopes, turning onto the road to Aráhova. Not another car in sight. Here Oedipus killed his father. Shadows throng on the earth.

•

(2) At Delphi the oracle spoke clearly and rationally, perhaps in verse, and directly to the inquirer, giving advice on matters of protocol and procedure, the likely course for the best results. Or pure echo function: ratification of plans already decided upon, like the Attorney General on Iraq. No evidence for afflatus, mania, inebriation, fumes, any kind of wildness (the instance in Plutarch was reported precisely because it was exceptional). Nor any extraordinary utterances or equivocal predictions, no ambiguity, no sphinx responses – these 'of folkloric origin', or historicised myths. / The stranger who leapt up from the side of the road. // And thousands of people each day from all over the world, aware to a greater or lesser extent where they are, or what they see: more stones, more nuthatches, snakes concealed in tales of gold. / The Cephalian Spring closed, gate locked, fenced off – there have been rock falls, and we wouldn't want anyone to be hurt, would we. Anyone in the world.

•

(2a) The discussion on the Syphnian Frieze: what must be said, passionately and immediately, for the nation depends on it / bodies signalling like letters on a page, the arm strikes a line between the organs of perception, back and forth. Like a line of poetry channelled to the soul and back. Everything we have, entrusted to a straight line, a direction, anywhere in the world. Until the crisis is past.

•

(3) A ferry over dark, blue, grey, sea – Egyio, Diakófto, and a slow drive up into the hills . . . / Dear Rough Guide, You will be interested to hear that the two hotels next door to each other at Zakhloroú, of which you recommend the one called Romantzo, are now both called Romantzo . . . / Zakhloroú, 8th February 1944: about 20 men. A small moss-grown memorial in the middle of a small public lawn / Kalávryta, half past two, 13th December 1943: 1,258 males over the age of 13. The church clock stopped.

•

(4) The mountain railway not running today, the cloud base coming down and lifting again and again, among the pines and rock slopes. Another monastery, 17th century crucifixes with minutely detailed wood carving, speaking of immense skill. What kind of wood? / The speech which springs directly from the earth's width, which creates its own usage to meet the possibility, to know what forces obtain, what is to be done. The speech that actually speaks, in words, pitches, arms, numbers, things. In minutely carved olive-wood. / A road-side stall selling honey at a remote corner in the hills, in the mist. Try it, he says, taste it. A malt-like streaked honey with an addictive aroma. It is from those trees over there, he says. Maybe spruce. / What is to be done? // Ancient Sykion. At last. Acres of foundation ruins among brown grass, on the slope from a low ridge. The clear picture, the better articulation, the linear spread. Lord it is lonesome among poor remnants of success, struggling to recognise the world.

II

Lying there in the darkness, what do you see? / Darkness, and traces of two windows to left and right, attained by starlight and the street lamps far across the valley. And hear, in the half hours, a local silence. // A street map of districts of north-west England: Stockport, Didsbury, Marple, Aigburth, Macclesfield, flickering through sleep, with their persons. I see the streets I hear the persons. Following the streets one by one. Following the old streets out of the world.

•

Readers, customers, friends and supporters, I'm trying to drive you all out of this paragraph. I need it for myself. As a dark space with two vague presences resembling windows. There to welcome the dead, to trace their journeys, marking the shallow sides of the path in the sandy earth. 'Withdraw, and separate.' And together we'll lament the frailty of the classics. And when the time comes, stand up and say, Well, I'll be going now. Shake hands, walk outside, and jump onto a bicycle.

•

Wandering the shore at Lerna again, thin band of stones nibbled by the sea, wire fences. // Another night map, basement flats in London in the 1950s, where promises are made which last the rest of a life / whose fracture spreads through lives . . . / 1920s, the young Ezra with his malevolence: 'but-not-altogether-satisfactory' which lasted a lifetime, his technique, crafted to hurt like a fine blade, beauty as incision // But the promises which you are born into and cannot step outside of, then 'beauty is admissible / and the love that creates it', the / benevolence, is this possible? / 'In beauty is deceit' (but not malevolence) *Why should I climb the look out?* // A spring flowing straight into the sea / deep, clear water, with trees.

•

Autumn, the welcome cold. It rains, the fields begin to show green. / In the dance the hands forming letters, like the letters on flowers / cursive / Arabic letters inscribed in the facial features, where a Sufi will read messages from God // 'When I saw the new Roman inscriptions I was full of apprehension. The letters had taken the forms of buildings: they were temples, markets, houses, gateways, mills, shops, columns . . . in lines on the stone page.' // How to begin, from the slightness we know we are, and the promise we inherit, and work towards truth, unarmed. / But we did, and a sweet forgetting ruled, dancing with signs for hands like the signs on flower heads, winter hands in hand over the strata, singing us / back to / where we began. / All the guns of providence were ablaze.

•

Arkadia

(1) in Arcadia, in / Dear Rough Guide, You will be distressed to learn that the Hotel Trikolonion at Stemnitsa, described (p.261) as family-run, very pleasant and hospitable, and reasonable in price, has, alas, fallen into the hands of the people with too much money. It was bought about a year ago by an outfit called Country Club Luxury Hotels and has been completely done over. Plate glass doors, stench of new leather, smart young person at counter . . . Cheapest available room in October 130 euros! A disaster. / So then in / whose Arcadia? Whose justice?

•

(2) 'To understand survival logic, poverty is essential.' The upturned palm, that Arcadia. // Monastéri Podrómou / stuck to a cliff-face like a swallow's nest. / We would like to stay the night here, it is possible, but the monk in charge will not speak to me, I am ignored and hang around the place like a ghost nobody believes in, entering the shrouded cave-church, hung with gold, turned inwards to its dark muscular centre. / Whose peace? Whose reward? The dark heart at the centre.

•

(3) The dark mind, the dark chemicals. Listening for the greatest possible distance. The approach of, / 'not a deity, but a substance, to be inhabited' / Whose work, whose truth?

•

(4) Withdraw and separate. The bar in Zátouna. Also general store, café, barber, hardware, agricultural implements, pictures, music . . . Where Theodorakis lay low for three years. / Gorge 500m deep with monasteries and hermitages stuck to its sides, hill towns higher up where it spreads out, the remains of a working mediaeval economy scattered all over it, all depending on water coming down from springs. Grain mills, fulling tubs, tanneries, wine vats, silk mills, all connected by mule tracks. Small stone-edged wheat fields on comparatively level stretches at the top. Village communism, independence. Withdrawn and separated. Resistance. / The pictures on the wall. 'My father the bouzouki player.'

•

(5) . . . over the Arkadian mountains, passing Karkaloú, possible site of ancient Th[e]isoa with a sanctuary to Zeus [Pausanias]. A little plateau approaching the summit of the pass, farm buildings among orchard trees, red ribbons on the corners of the house. // The answering, the brightened heart, a refuge because a resource, and a resilience, a burgeoning, a dazzling sanity / Trees on the turn, bees on the urn, the flying birds on the top corners of the lanarkes (clay coffins) in the museum at Thiva / amateur heart tracing the hopes of death / Pick it up by the corners and fly away with it, the poor being, the forgotten name. Turn out to sea with it, and off for the islands. The white crowns floating on the springs.

•

And all our ghosts will assemble / along the sides of the route, shining through the night, leading us home / We have it all, we have it all to heart in its bits and pieces / look / at it there, the plurality shining in the night / seeking questions for its answers.

•

Coming again to the Argive Heraion, where gain and loss, night and day, question and answer, are all flattened. The hard ground thick with little purple flowers on bare stems, bees busy among them, bee-loud ground, among small trees and foundation stones. Aromatic herbs heavy in the air, from such thin cover, the earth unconcealed. // The joining powers diminish, the fat things fade / to float a stone slab on the dry terraces.

III

Living under an unjust war, which can only create more wars. And to speak of 'democracy' and keep secrets from your people. Governance serves 'the business community', makes up international law as it goes along. Uncontrolled speculation blanches the fields. People are frightened, parsimony turns aggressive // *Cloudy weather, the sun refuse to shine / Some old day, your troubles be like mine / Where on earth you go.* Fingernail on wire. Dead voices, responding. Denying everything I say.

•

We held our opposition for so long, so defiantly, up in the hills until it seemed that what we opposed had scattered itself into the land and melted into the landscape and it was time to return and claim the vacant home / and this was our victory, in the sellotape and sausages and plumbing and wiring and the writing of 'Everyday Life' / our nameless country. Ring of hammer on metal, spectral music.

•

I put on a CD of Byzantine church song, it says / 'Christ is risen' / But risen as what, it doesn't say. A justice, a redemption, an umbrella, an aerial? // The representation in stone of wind-blown silk, or wisps of hair, impossible for a thousand years / and the secular complexity devolving on hope / the lyric of everyday, our actual spatial engagement / obscured, for a thousand years? / A possibility kept alive in ephemeral heresies and desert monasteries / A stake in the world, a dry stick thrust into the sandy soil on the edge of a migration route and / twisted and twirled into depth.

•

Pull all these things together, pull them onto, the single image / the stone in the road, that small flower /// withdrew the dedication to Napoleon and tore out the title-page.

•

A point at which reward of any kind is abandoned. / 1850s, exiles from all over Europe in London, weeping failed revolutions / / I suddenly remembered the small monastery on the main road between Florence and Fiesole where you could ring a bell to see a Botticelli crucifixion. We were shown in by an old monk of quiet, genial disposition who coped well with our poor Italian. He showed us the fresco, and the vegetable garden in a cloister, and said, 'There are twelve monks here, of whom nine are dying.' *How do we see our way through this darkness?* / Closing both eyes, like opening a book, and seeing. And what do you see? / People.

•

People of whom nothing remains. Peasants, builders, workers, suppliers, teachers, who kept the thing going while the governors panicked / and whose songs were real songs, lyric, not those vast chains of proprietorship catalogues of brutality and reasons for entitlement to free dinners / but movements of grace on the offered instant / which survive / as the flowers in the vase survive from vase to vase, year to year, flower to flower, yellow red and purple clustered in the sun.

•

Beauty comes and goes / and obeys the whip-end, turns by the moon pale and full / turning to a new tune / The coats of cattle like scattered leaves across the slopes, / orchids, rusty dolls on stalks. Does / not beauty then, the hard and distinct differentiation which / it is, does it not then / necessitate a certain aggression? / Warming the home heart by allotting decline and death to the outsider / temporarily, is it, in the / moment? / I don't know. The thin kine picking a sustenance on dry plains, with coats like emperors' robes.

•

Athens
(1) Ring dove in the park, I throw a crisp at it, it / doesn't want it. This is true democracy.

•

(2) The Pnyx: a democracy, a concave auditorium, inverse of theatre / The Attic grave stelae at the Keramicos: the floating baby, the final handshake, the downcasting, wisps of hair raised in the breeze / The gates of the city, where there is always a fountain. // Bring it all to the one image, where we are. We are at a backpacker hostel with a help-yourself hot water urn for instant coffee in the morning. / But the messages in the air which encompass all this detail and draw the species together – we breathe them in, like poetry. / Remember, they say, the tombstones, the fountains, right of asylum. Remember the words we don't use any more. 'A democracy to silver the land.'

•

(3) Dear Rough Guide, Some of the eating places you recommend in Plaka are little more than dens of food bandits. One you don't mention is Kapnikaréa, tucked away in a corner of the square of the same name. They don't give the stuff away but it's good food at reasonable prices for the area, casual, friendly, and seems to have impromptu live bouzouki music from about 2 p.m. / People doing things well. If you can't find it in poetry look for it somewhere else.

•

Last bus to Argos. The day sinking away, small lights emerging in the hillsides, among the olive trees. A town centre at some distance, clusters of luminous blue and yellow flickering through trees. Distance itself, welcoming itself to the heart from somewhere, nobody knows where, from Asia. Flames leaping from an old oil drum in the corner of a factory yard, consuming the day's residue.

•

Trouble in mind / Awaiting a return / (of ? / / socialism, peace, honour, justice. Words we don't use. Freedom. / Living in anxiety. 'If the people are unhappy, the dead will return and try again.' / Ghost nation, your delicate air, world hidden in world, concordance of ear and eye. / One word, shouted in the night, whispered along the arm, restores the nation of sense, word out of word / The bay below, cloud on the sea at dawn, the hills emerging like islands, the sea hidden in the sea.

•

Bright sunlight, sharpening the edges of the house, the blazing secret of it, the day. / A reason for coming here. And gathering messages from petals on the stony hillsides and the feathers of birds in flight, and small moths hesitating on grass stalks. / The hopes and fears of peoples, cast on the sea shattered into particles of light

•

And bounding the inhabited zone in a musical tone, from some contraption or other, radio, flute, goat bell, disco . . . The song, a / simple thing, but which has to keep moving / uphill, the pull back from gravitation as from speed and the lone ranger stalks the plains / / You know this, wherever you are, you hear the faint tone / the onomatopoeic bird-name signalling the entrance to the silence of ever. The apples shining on the far away tree.

•

Up there looking down / on the Argive Heraion, which is almost nothing. Stone lines, a medlar tree, edge of fallen wall, in the late haze. A slightness fermenting at peace, richer than negation or gain. A dream-breaking stranger in the mind for ever after. / 'We will outshine the sun'.

10 Postludes
ExoMáni 2005

Arriving at dawn in the foothills of Taigétos / the dark shapes becoming known, sense / unfolding from the eastward slopes, a little misty, beginning to breathe / A golden jackal crosses the road / the recurrent beginning of more than a day if the lost brother returns the hormonal bandit is forgiven and / down into the waking streets, slow beetle of dawn, the light fills. Peace is promised by the very earth: an end to your long duties.

•

Dancing in from the sea in a sun column, human gratification / The martins dipping over the harbour, their intricately structured lives / darting to and from mud nests under the balcony, acts which adorn their own philosophy, their shrill call / / We are bent to our inhering promise as the song is raised above the waves to venture forth, to trust the stranger, currently asleep in the bar, who will one day re-establish the heart's true, stone-set, perimeter. / There is also a small bull grazing salt on the stone shore . . . / Europe enters Asia with lowered eyes, clutching a begging bowl. Rice or forgiveness, whatever you can spare.

•

(a) Whitethroated sea / discursive light / pale red wine holding / a gleam in the glass / Dionysiac calm.

(b) The little owls that live in holes in the walls of the tower, busy all night and most of the day.

(c) Intermittent bursts of warm wind all night shaking the dry leaves like waves breaking. Lying in darkness in the small stone house listening, slowly submitting, waiting.

(d) Dionysiac silence and stillness, Cretan thoughts / that any length of time fully furnished runs with the moonslick towards the encompassing arm, all its facets conjoined.

•

Kranaï, now called Marathonísi, 'Isle of Fennel', opposite, on the shore, the Sanctuary of Aphrodite Migonitis, 'of the lovers' embrace'. The fire carried over the mountains in a small pouch or a piece of fennel stalk. / Here Helen and Paris ratified their love, in an arch-shaped discourse if / you believe it, if you wish // Up in the hills, fortress villages, stone cubes clustered on ridge ends, door locked or gone. / The constant wind beyond the thick wall at night. Safety and love pursued / to a point where you do not wish any longer, but know / the little circuits of blood / will never cease their journeying.

•

Arching over all that epic tension, the little owls go about their businesses. The two falcons screaming over the cliffs towards Trachila, courting or fighting in great parabolas / And those lovers, who sailed out from the white harbour, secure in their domestic purpose, tending their day, towards a new home under the sun's eye // The dry grasses scrape in the night breeze / with messages of slightness and absence, and I am more than ever / bound to it, the death letter, *grinnin in your face.* / And it will, you know it will, the boat moving out from the harbour taking us both with it. The little owls know it too, shouting love through the dark stone.

•

Deep Mani

(a) To Cape Ténaron, one of the ends of the earth. Where is the city, we say, where are the ruins, the mosaic, the temple? I can't see anything but stony hillsides falling to the sea. Where is the entrance to Hades? All ends of the earth are entrances to Hades.

(b) Forsaken land, prison land, fortress villages. To get away from the sun, its optimism and welcome, hate it, hide from it in stone cells with tiny windows: an aristocracy. / An unlocked door in one of the towers of Vathia, an iron bed and a wooden chair and a lot of grey dust / someone's office, someone's tomb // O you can shake it you can break it you can stick it on the wall the truth is always ever wider and brighter than it was.

(c) Retreat to hotel on sea front, windows flung open (Yerolimín). Sun's red eye in the bay. Evening gathers, the rocks cast whiteness into the air. Well-being, handled so much better by poverty than by wealth, through mutual aid and then it is moral: red snapper in lemon sauce.

(d) Sitting silently in the churchyard at Haronda, stone bench in west front. White walls, forming across the yard a house or raised room in which someone perhaps lives, there is an electricity box on the wall, and a light at the top of the steps / but at present no person to be found, some small bird raising hell in the bushes across the road. / No person, no answer. For as long as we live. We travel so far, again and again, and we wait where nothing will arrive, and in that pause is a book, a learned book, putting itself together, a mosaic. Conversing with the dead at another entrance to Hades, continuous with the sky.

•

Such fair darkness, such deeply infused light / Time, halt a while your pressing / Deep blue almost black of / the slender rock-thrush / standing on a rock / on the edge of the sea // The mind dances on words / on the edge of nothing / to the delight of the blind and the lame, who join the dance / and see the blue rock-thrush / on the edge of the sea.

•

Out across the flowery fields, white flowers and some blue, hanging on thin stems, the cover already dried yellow in late spring / bees and wasps hard at work all day / The equitable, evident, persistent, fair floweriness of the fields / until we approach a 'property' O how / the dogs to bark!

•

Helen scattered everywhere, setting that foot on the shore: Troy, Egypt, Pephnos, Yíthion, islands . . . // In the deep light of early evening blood is on the move, there are meetings / under the lamp-post, on the corner of the street, a certain little lady / the light that holds us, lady light, burning in the night, attracting moths, missiles, dry old souls fluttering at the window // Until that final, safe, island, in the Black Sea, where the record is maintained. And lyric redeems narrative, and hand in hand on the edge of the sand . . . / The small boat entering the harbour, turning the engine off, drifting to the quayside, carrying home, by the light of the moon.

•

The dream of awakedness / a little shell against / death's advance / Walking in the slight rain, thunder up in the hills / blue-tinted white flowers in the brown fields sharpened under moisture // The boat comes in the catch is unloaded the man goes home to sleep / as dawn unburdens the coast. Take us / there, where side by side the swimming souls delight together in renewed trust / we live there and always shall / one after another, the truth shell, that / holding thing, against / death's rush.

Some topographical notes

Mani sections:

The site is on the west coast of the Peloponnese, with mainland Greece and ultimately what is now called Asia at our backs beyond the mountains. Sense of movement in *Greek Passages* inhabits an east-west tension and always implies its contrary, as in a trade, with hints of resolution or disruption outside this linearity. The first three pieces establish the east-west contra-passage but 'sky falcon' and 'dawn beetle' are both Egyptian (southern) terms, and, for instance, during the later course of the work many northern entities (memories, armies etc.), invade the dream.

Local rumour, aided and abetted by Kelvin Corcoran, places exactly at the spot where we stayed (a tiny isthmus with a 17th Century tower on it, a harbour, and a few houses) the embarkment of Helen and Paris for Troy, having travelled over the hills from Kranaï (setting out westwards to travel east).

The island in the Black Sea: Leuke, the White Island, in the estuary of the Donau, where 'Passing sailors could hear Achilles and Helen at night, singing the story of their lives in the verses of Homer.' Peter Levi, notes to his translation of Pausanias (1979) summarising Philostratus.

Argolid sections:

The home site here overlooks the head of the Bay of Argos which was the principal point of arrival for sea traffic from East and South to Mycenae and the other early palace-citadels scattered round the head of the bay: Argos, Tiryns, Asine, Midea.

The story referred to in the third piece and dispersed throughout is the plot of Aeschylus' *The Suppliants*.

Lerna is an archaeological site to the west side of the Bay of Argos, next to the village of Mili, the foundations of a Neolithic house close to the sea. There is a bounteous spring beside it which is identified as the Lerna where Hercules fought the Hydra, one of the entrances to Hades; but so is the great lake or swamp of Lerna, now a flat agricultural area crossed by several waterways at the head of the bay about 5km away.

The 'watchtower' is a small big-stone ruin in the village of Elleniko known as the 'pyramid', of unknown function but possibly an outlook over the bay.

Palestinian wedding party: it was an occasional news item several years ago that a Palestinian wedding celebration at which guns were fired into the air late at night, a frequent custom in traditional societies which use guns and still observed in rural Greece, had alarmed the Israeli army who had shelled the event, killing most of those involved.

Cycladic figures were deposited in tombs lying on their backs, possibly representing the dead and were originally painted with facial and bodily features.

Radio Tarifa is a Spanish musical group working in an eclectic style based on the congruence of pan-Mediterranean traditions.

Mykines is Greek for Mycenae and is the name of the modern village near to it.

The 1940s dates and quantities of persons (executed) in the Gulf of Korinth section, refer of course to the activities of the German occupying forces. The number I give for Kalávrita is one of six different counts I have found, varying from 511 to 1,436.

The Argive Heraion: the mother of all temples.

Things read in the autumn of 2003 which are particularly informative to the first half of Greek Passages –

Aeschylus, *The Suppliants*.
Helmut Baumann, *Greek Wild Flowers and the Plant Lore of Ancient Greece*, 1993.
Roberto Calasso, *The Marriage of Cadmus and Harmony*, 1994.
Peter Levi, *The Hill of Kronos*, 1980.
R. Gordon Wasson, Albert Hoffman and Carl A.P. Ruck, *The Road to Eleusis*, 1978.

Information on sheep bells from The Museum of Greek Musical Instruments, Athens.

And things read in the autumn of 2004 and spring of 2005 which are involved in the second half –

Marguerite Poland, *Iron Love*, 1999 and *Recessional for Grace*, 2003 (novels).
David H. Turner, *Return to Eden, a journey through the promised landscape of Amagalyuagba*, 1989.
The information on Delphi was from Joseph Fontenrose, *The Delphic Oracle*, 1978.
There are several quotations from the songs of Frank Stokes and Uncle Dave Macon.

And throughout–

Pausanias, The Guide to Greece, translated by Peter Levi. Revised edition, 1979.

www.ingramcontent.com/pod-product-compliance
Lightning Source LLC
Chambersburg PA
CBHW031155160426
43193CB00008B/369